WALKS FOR ALL AGES
DARTMOOR

WALKS *FOR*
ALL AGES

DARTMOOR

JOHN NOBLET

BRADWELL
BOOKS

Published by Bradwell Books
11 Orgreave Close Sheffield S13 9NP
Email: books@bradwellbooks.co.uk

British Library Cataloguing in Publication Data: a catalogue record for this book is available from the British Library.

1st Edition

ISBN: 9781909914155

Print: Gomer Press, Llandysul, Ceredigion SA44 4JL

Design by: Erik Siewko Creative, Derbyshire.
eriksiewko@gmail.com

Photograph Credits: © John Noblet

Maps: Contain Ordnance Survey data
© Crown copyright and database right 2014

Ordnance Survey licence number 100039353

The information in this book has been produced in good faith and is intended as a general guide. Bradwell Books and its authors have made all reasonable efforts to ensure that the details are correct at the time of publication. Bradwell Books and the author cannot accept any responsibility for any changes that have taken place subsequent to the book being published. It is the responsibility of individuals undertaking any of the walks listed in this publication to exercise due care and consideration for the health and wellbeing of each other in the party. Particular care should be taken if you are inexperienced. The walks in this book are not especially strenuous but individuals taking part should ensure they are fit and able to complete the walk before setting off.

CONTENTS

INTRODUCTION

DARTMOOR IS A VERY SPECIAL PLACE AND IS SOMETIMES CALLED 'ENGLAND'S LAST GREAT WILDERNESS'. ON DARTMOOR, YOU CAN BE FURTHER FROM A ROAD THAN ANYWHERE ELSE IN ENGLAND.

The National Park covers an area of 365 square miles. This high, sometimes wild, moorland is the highest land south of the Peak District. It has a wealth of history and there is evidence of four thousand years of human activity at every turn. There are Bronze Age (2000 BC to 500 BC) stone rows, stone circles and hut complexes, tinners' workings from the Middle Ages (13th and 14th centuries) and later 19th-century industrial remains to be seen on almost every walk.

There are many ancient trackways across the moor that are hundreds of years old. Some originate from the pre-Reformation abbeys at Tavistock, Buckfast and Buckland whilst others connected the Stannary towns of the medieval tin mining industry. Some are named, such as the Abbot's Way, the Jobber's Path and the Lych Way, and are still marked by ancient bridges and waymarking crosses.

Dartmoor is, however, much more than just a wild open space. There are rivers that flow to the north to find their way to the Bristol Channel and rivers that flow south to the English Channel. There are picturesque villages and ancient towns, each with its own individual character. Flora and fauna are varied with ancient woodlands and heather-clad moors. The indigenous and iconic ponies can be found in many areas whilst buzzards and skylarks soar overhead.

Legends abound. Many stories, such as the Hound of the Baskervilles and Uncle Tom Cobley, are based on fact. Others require more imagination but are part of what makes Dartmoor unique.

The walks in this book aim to show a snapshot of all that the moor has to offer. There are walks on the wild side, in river valleys and around some of the towns and villages. The 'must see' places such as Haytor and Widecombe, Postbridge and Princetown are included.

Walkers are, however, reminded that the upland areas of Dartmoor are open and exposed and care needs to be taken. In particular:

- Although the walks have been chosen as suitable for all ages, sensible stout walking shoes, ideally light walking boots, are essential.

- Weather conditions can change rapidly. In all but the most settled conditions waterproofs should be taken.

- Most of Dartmoor is 'open access' land, i.e. there is 'a right to roam'. However, some areas are privately owned and there may not be a right of access. Dartmoor is still very much a working environment, particularly farming and military use.

- Visitors need to be aware that there are three areas of Dartmoor that are used by the military for training purposes. These are clearly marked on OS maps as 'Danger Areas' and access is sometimes restricted. Details are published in advance and red flags are flown, but only one walk in this book is within such an area.

- Mobile phone coverage is generally poor.

- Sat nav postcodes are given for the start point of each walk. However, as Dartmoor is sparsely populated these are only approximate. Grid references are also provided, which provide a more accurate location.

1 HAYTOR

THIS IS A GENTLE AND VARIED WALK, STEPPING BACK IN TIME AND LOOKING AT LONG-FORGOTTEN INDUSTRIES AND TRANSPORT SYSTEMS. IT IS IN THE SHADOW OF THE ICONIC HAYTOR ROCKS AND HAS FAR-REACHING VIEWS TO THE SEA.

There are many reminders of granite quarrying along this walk, the most important (and unusual) being the Haytor Granite Tramway, built in 1820 by George Templer. The route of this tramway is now known as the Templer Way and was originally used to convey granite from the Haytor quarries to the terminus of the Stover Canal, 1300 ft (400m) lower. The Stover Canal had been built in 1792 by George's father, James, to carry clay for export from his land near Kingsteignton. The granite was then transferred to barges on the canal and taken to Teignmouth for loading on to sea-going ships.

At various points along the way you will see remains of the track on which the trucks ran. These are unique in that they were formed of granite sections shaped to guide the wheels of the horse-drawn wagons. The wagons had plain iron wheels without flanges which meant that they could be manoeuvred at the terminals more easily. Teams of horses, as many as 18, pulled the loaded trucks up from the quarries but then gravity took over for the seven-mile journey to the canal basin. The empty trucks were then pulled back up by the horses.

At the start of the walk you will pass Moorlands on your right. Originally The Moorlands Hotel, the setting inspired Agatha Christie to write her first book, The Mysterious Affair at Styles. Shortly after you will come across a row of cottages and a pub, now called the Rock Inn, built in 1825 for the quarry workers.

We follow the tramway up onto Haytor Down and will see Hound Tor in the distance, said to be part of the inspiration for Sir Arthur Conan Doyle to write The Hound of the Baskervilles.

Towards the end of the walk you will be able to explore one of the old quarries, now flooded. It is an eerie place but well worth a visit. It is full of wildlife and there are some interesting remains of old machinery.

Afterwards, take a look around the Visitor Centre which has more on the history of the Templer Way and the Haytor quarries.

THE BASICS

Distance: 3 miles / 4.75km

Gradient: Gentle

Severity: Easy

Time: 1¾ hours

Stiles: None

Map: OS Explorer OL28 (Dartmoor)

Path description: Moorland paths and a quiet lane

Start point: Haytor Dartmoor National Park Information Centre (GR SX 765772)

Parking: Pay and display car park adjacent to Visitor Centre (TQ13 9XP)

Dog friendly: Yes, but on leads on public road or near animals on the moor

Public toilets: At start

Nearest food: Seasonal snack bar in car park. Rock Inn at Haytor Vale

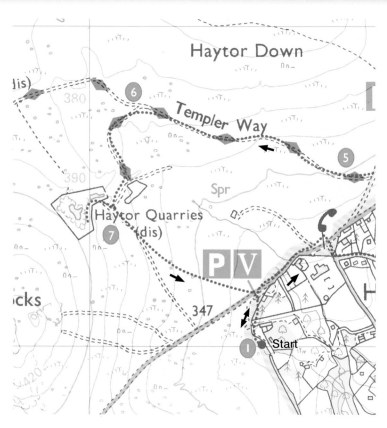

THE ROUTE

1. With your back to the Information Centre, carefully cross the road, turn right and walk along the grassy verge. Pass the entrance to Moorlands, where there is a café on your return, and after approximately 300m turn right at the phone box (signed Haytor Vale). Go over the cattle grid and immediately turn left and walk down the hill.

2. Where the road bends to the right, turn left onto a public bridleway just before reaching the Rock Inn. After a

As officers, they were allowed to walk around but boundary stones were set up which marked the limit to which they could go.

Allow time after the walk to have a stroll around the village itself. The Church House, now owned by the National Trust, is one of the finest examples of a 16th-century church house, originally used for parish festivities or 'ales'. There are two pubs and tea shops as well.

THE BASICS

Distance: 4 miles / 6.5km

Gradient: A steady climb, steep in part, to Chinkwell Tor. Easy return on a quiet lane

Severity: Hard at first, then easy

Time: 2¼ hours

Stiles: None

Map: OS Explorer OL28 (Dartmoor)

Path description: Lanes and moorland paths

Start point: Widecombe village green (GR SX 719769)

Parking: Widecombe car park. Pay & display April to October (TQ13 7TA)

Dog friendly: Yes, but on leads if near animals on the moor or on public roads

Public toilets: At start

Nearest food: Cafés and pubs in Widecombe

2 WIDECOMBE IN THE MOOR WALK

THE ROUTE

1. Turn left out of the car park and walk down the hill past Wayside Café and Mill House. Be careful as this road can be busy. After 200m cross the stone bridge over a small stream and turn left.

2. Walk along this quiet lane which soon crosses the East Webburn River on another bridge. Bell Tor appears ahead as the lane starts to climb towards the hamlet of Bonehill. Pass Lower Bonehill Farm on the right (note the huge boulders in the garden) and then Middle Bonehill on the left. These are both examples of Devon longhouses. A longhouse is a traditional Dartmoor farmhouse. The living quarters were at one end of the building and the animals were kept at the other end. One has the date 1682 over the door. The hill steepens as a small stream tumbles alongside.

3. At the moor gate stop to catch your breath and admire the views back towards Widecombe and beyond. Turn left up the stony track with a wall on the left but bear right after only 50m to follow a grassy path going to the right of Bell Tor. Continue onwards and upwards towards Chinkwell Tor, where the views really open up. On the right are Rippon Tor, Saddle Tor and the distinctive double summit of Haytor Rocks. On the left is the almost level ridge of Hameldown. There are several grassy tracks near the top but keep left to walk towards the cairn piles on the summit which is 458m (1502ft) above sea level. Now you can see Hound Tor on the right with the lower outline of Hayne Down to the left (or north) of it. If you look carefully at the far left end you should be able to see the profile of Bowerman's Nose and, on a clear day, on the horizon, the sea near Teignmouth.

4. There are two cairns on the summit, possibly ancient burial places now marked by piles of stones. Go between the two stone piles and then down on the grassy track towards Honeybag Tor. Note the small pond to the right of the track known as Slades Well. In the dip, just before climbing up to Honeybag Tor, take the grassy path on the left going downhill beside an old gulley, possibly a tin working, and a few solitary hawthorn trees. (It is worth climbing up to the top of Honeybag Tor to see the many strange-shaped rocks on the summit).

5. Fork right near the bottom and then go right on a stony track. Go through a gate and continue down this track, now rather rough, to the road by a cattle grid.

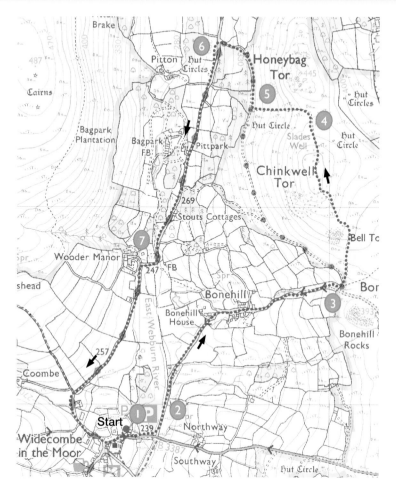

6. Turn left and walk down this lane with the East Webburn River in the valley below. As you pass a substantial house at Bagpark you should see alpacas in the field beside the road.

7. Shortly after this (about 200m from the entrance gates to Bagpark) look out for a small stream tumbling out of the roadside wall on the left. Almost opposite this is the parole stone. The curious spelling of '1 miol' is no doubt due to the way that word was spoken in those times by the locals. Continue down the lane past fields and woodlands which are full of bluebells in spring. In Widecombe bear left at the village green to reach the car park. The church is well worth a visit as is the adjoining Church House (National Trust) on your return.

3 PARKE & BOVEY TRACEY

A WOODLAND WALK THAT IS GREAT AT ANY TIME OF THE YEAR.
IT IS MOSTLY IN THE NATIONAL TRUST'S PARKE ESTATE AND WE
FOLLOW THE RIVER BACK ALONG AN OLD RAILWAY LINE. THE
EASY OPTIONAL EXTENSION ALLOWS YOU TO EXPLORE BOVEY
TRACEY.

Our walk starts in the grounds of Parke, which was owned by the Hole family. They built the Georgian manor house in the 1820s. The house is now the headquarters of the Dartmoor National Park Authority but the surrounding parkland and woods are freely open to the public.

Within the grounds of Parke is the Dartmoor Pony Heritage Trust visitor and education centre. This charity was set up to protect the native Dartmoor pony. The centre is open to the public (free, but a donation is requested) during the summer months.

After walking through some delightful beech woodland our path drops down to the River Bovey at Wilsford Bridge. At this point we meet the track bed of the former Newton Abbot to Moretonhampstead railway.

This section of the walk is between the stations of Bovey (not Bovey Tracey, according to the railway) and Lustleigh. Below Bovey Tracey the line was built on part of the route of the Haytor Granite Tramway, which features in another walk in this book.

Of modest size as rivers go, the River Bovey flows from the eastern side of Dartmoor through Lustleigh Cleave to Bovey Tracey to join the River Teign. The river gives its name to the Bovey Basin, which is a major source in the UK of ball clay. Ball clay is a fine ceramic clay and, confusingly, produces better quality porcelain than the more common china clay which is found on the western side of Dartmoor.

After an easy stroll through the woods with the river below, the shorter walk returns to Parke. Another mile along this old railway will, however, bring you to the old town of Bovey Tracey.

Bovey Tracey is mentioned in the Domesday Book and the name derives from the River Bovey and the de Tracey family who were lords of the manor after the Norman Conquest. There is a good mixture of shops and several tea shops and pubs. The Devon Guild of Craftsmen have their headquarters in the mid-19th-century Riverside Mill which is well worth a visit.

THE BASICS

Distance: 2½ miles / 4km or 4 miles / 6.5km

Gradient: Gentle gradients in woods with two moderate descents

Severity: Moderate

Time: 1½ or 2 hours

Stiles: None

Map: OS Explorer OL28 (Dartmoor)

Path description: Meadow and woodland paths to a quiet lane and returning on an old railway track. The optional riverside path is uneven and possibly muddy in parts

Start point: Parke (GR SX 805785) Parke is just outside Bovey Tracey on the B3387 road to Haytor

Parking: National Trust pay and display car park (TQ13 9LE)

Dog friendly: Yes, if under control

Public toilets: At start and in Bovey Tracey on the longer walk

Nearest food: Home Farm Café at Parke. Pubs and cafés in Bovey Tracey

THE ROUTE

1. From the bottom left corner of the National Trust car park take the path on the left just before the gate and information board signed "Orchard and red walk trail". (The orchard is on the right: just go through the gate to see it).

    Go through a field gate and continue on a track across a grassy field alongside a fence through two more gates (but turn around to admire the views over Bovey Tracey and to Newton Abbot behind you). Bear left to cross a second grassy field to a kissing gate in the far corner leading into Blackmoor Copse.

2. Descend through the woods and just before a stile leading to a lane turn right to descend further. After a series of steps carry on to a path junction. Turn left to meet a lane by two substantial houses.

3. Turn right on the lane to reach Wilsford Bridge over the River Bovey.

    Pass under an old railway bridge, now part of a recreational route known as the Wrey Valley Trail. Coming fairly late in the railway mania years, this railway was opened in 1866 and was operated at that time by the South Devon Railway Company. Subsequently absorbed by the Great Western Railway (GWR) and

    closed in 1959 the line followed the valleys of the rivers Teign and Bovey.

    There were never more than eight passenger trains a day but there was also one goods train, usually for cattle and agricultural produce.

    After the old railway bridge immediately turn right through a wooden gate back into the National Trust Parke estate and up a short slope to reach the track bed, now a footpath.

4. Here there is a choice. The easiest way back is along the old railway. Walk along with the river on the right, passing under a bridge after a while.

5. At a path junction that is signed to the car park (just before reaching a Gothic looking house behind a substantial timber fence) turn right down the slope to the meadow to return to Parke. Go over the old stone bridge (Parke Bridge) and continue on the good track to a path crossing by a timber farm building.

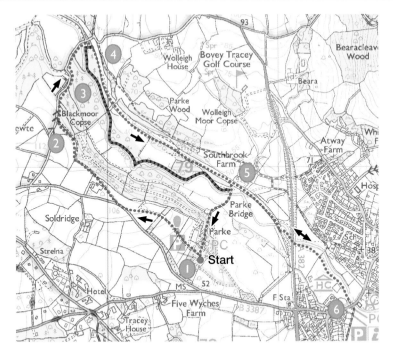

Go straight on, up the short hill and then left through a white gate at the top. Where the path forks, go right between stone buildings to the yard (where you will find the toilets and a small display of farm wagons). Go up the steps beside the toilets to the café, then left up the drive and back to the car park.

Riverside path option: If you prefer to walk alongside the river, cross the old railway track at waypoint 4 and go down the slope on the far side. Turn left alongside the river, eventually passing through two kissing gates and later a weir. Soon after this the path reaches a meadow. At the far end of this is Parke Bridge as above. Turn right to return to Parke or left to regain the railway to continue to Bovey Tracey.

6. To visit Bovey Tracey, continue on the old railway at waypoint 5. Go over the river bridge and within a few metres fork left to walk alongside the river. Go under the road bridge to continue on a good path beside a sports ground and then a children's play area. The path meets the bottom of Bovey Tracey's main street. Almost opposite is the Riverside Mill, now the craft centre. Turn left for the town centre or right for a choice of teashops. Retrace your steps to waypoint 5 to return to Parke.

4 LUSTLEIGH

Lustleigh is a picture postcard village and surely one of the prettiest in the Dartmoor National Park. This walk combines thatched cottages with a woodland and riverside ramble through the famous Lustleigh Cleave, a national nature reserve.

Lustleigh Cleave (cleave means 'cliff' or 'cleft') is a geological feature known as a fault which has resulted in a deep-sided valley through which the River Bovey, a tributary of the River Teign, has carved its way.

Our walk starts in the centre of the village by the fine parish church which dates mostly from the 14th and 15th centuries. Nearby is the 15th-century thatched pub, appropriately called The Cleave, and there are a number of interesting old buildings, some thatched, clustered around the square.

The first part of the walk goes through the recreation park known as The Orchard which was given to the village as a public area in 1966. The largest of several granite boulders, topped by a granite throne, is used for the annual coronation of the May Queen. The story of the Lustleigh May Queen festival dates back to the 1300s. The people of Lustleigh escaped a plague epidemic and decided to celebrate their good fortune by holding festivities on May Day. The tradition died out but was revived in 1905 and has continued ever since, moving to this park in 1954. The names of the children carved on the boulder date from that time.

There is a fairly steep climb at first to the hamlet of Pethybridge with its thatched cottages. From here there are views back over Lustleigh, dominated by the church tower, and across the valley towards Kelly. At Kelly there is an old iron mine which operated on and off from the 1790s to 1951 and is occasionally open to the public.

The top of the hill is reached by way of an old green lane at Heaven's Gate. From here the track descends to Hisley Bridge, a fine old bridge over the River Bovey with low parapets to allow packhorses to cross.

Clifford Bridge was built in the 17th century but widened in 1821 unusually by extending either side, so that it is the centre part that is the oldest. The road was once the main route from Exeter to Chagford.

We walk a short distance on the now quiet lane before entering the Nature Reserve to walk back alongside the river.

THE BASICS

Distance: 6 miles / 9.5 km

Gradient: A steady climb and descent at first and then almost level

Severity: Moderate at first and then Easy

Time: 2¾ hours

Stiles: None

Map: OS Explorer 28 Dartmoor

Path description: Woodland and riverside tracks and paths

Start point: Steps Bridge

Parking: Free car park on the west side of Steps Bridge (GR SX 803883) EX6 7EQ

ouse Inn House Inn

Dog friendly: Yes

Public toilets: None

Nearest food: Seasonal tea rooms and pub in Dunsford 1 mile away

5 STEPS BRIDGE WALK

THE ROUTE

1. Cross the road from the car park and go up the concrete drive signed as a bridleway. Almost immediately continue straight on at a junction signed to St Thomas Cleave. The path climbs steadily through beech and oak woodland with glimpses of the Teign valley below to reach a gate. Soon the path levels out as it joins the track to Little Heltor Farm.

2. Cross the road with care and take the permissive bridleway signed again to St Thomas Cleave. Pass a junction and continue downwards into the cleave. Go straight on at another junction signed as a circular walk. The path drops steeply at first and then descends gradually towards the Doccombe Brook. Cross a footbridge and continue alongside the edge of the wood and a meadow.

3. Go left just past a ruined building, possibly an old mill, where there is a footbridge on the right. There is no sign but there is an information board and, just beyond that, a gate leading into Ross Meadow. Follow a path alongside the river marked by posts with green arrows. This meadow is being restored to encourage wildlife in general and butterflies in particular. At the end of the meadow go through a gate onto a track alongside the river.

4. A little further on the path forks, and another track goes uphill. However, keep right alongside the river signed to Clifford Bridge. After about ¾ mile (1.2km) the track passes a number of wooden chalets to reach a gate onto a lane. Continue ahead to a junction (but noticing a collection of old granite artefacts and a ruin, possibly another old mill, on the right). At the junction turn right to cross Clifford Bridge.

    (If you feel like a longer walk, you can go left at this junction, up the hill for a few metres and then right onto another riverside track that will take you all the way to Fingle Bridge)

5. After crossing Clifford Bridge continue to the crossroads at Clifford Cross. Turn right, signed for Dunsford. Follow this lane for nearly half a mile (700m) alongside the river to reach a sharp left hand bend. Just after the bend go through a gate on the right, signed as a bridlepath into Dunsford Nature Reserve. Cross a stream and turn right.

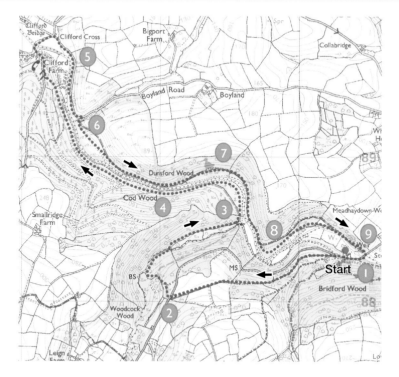

6. After a few metres take the right fork (rather than the bridlepath which is signed to the left). This path will take you past an information board and into a meadow which will be full of wild daffodils in early spring.

7. Where the path forks by another bridlepath sign go right again to keep close to the river. Cross a small footbridge and shortly after this, turn right at a path junction to continue alongside the river.

8. Once again, at a further bridleway sign go right to continue alongside the river bank. Getting close to Steps Bridge there is a weir. This is where the leat for Dunsford Mill, situated about 650m on the other side of the bridge, is taken off. Notice how it flows through a separate arch of the bridge. The weir does, in fact, incorporate the stepping stones which probably gave the bridge its name.

9. At the road turn right to cross the bridge. The bridge marks the boundary of Dunsford and Bridford parishes and the village names are carved on the parapets, one each side of the roadway. You can also see the date of its construction (1816). Continue up the road for 150m to reach the car park but please be careful, this can be a busy road.

6 CHAGFORD

A VERY VARIED WALK AROUND CHAGFORD. THERE ARE BIG VIEWS, A RIVERSIDE PATH AND AN INTERESTING SMALL MARKET TOWN TO EXPLORE AT THE END. ALTHOUGH THERE IS A STEEP CLIMB UP TO NATTADON COMMON AND SEVERAL STILES ON THIS WALK, THE EFFORT WILL BE WELL WORTH IT.

Chagford is an ancient town and some of the buildings in the centre, including the church of St Michael, date from the 16th century. Other buildings have links with the Civil War and the Pilgrim Fathers, one of the first groups to establish a colony in the New World. The quaint octagonal Market House in the main square is most unusual.

We leave Chagford by walking south along New Street – it was new once, many hundreds of years ago! After climbing to the top of Nattadon Common, over 1000 ft (300m) above sea level, you can catch your breath and admire the views. Behind are some of the higher tors of Dartmoor whilst ahead is the steep-sided valley of the River Teign and the mid-Devon countryside beyond.

We leave the high ground by following an old drovers' lane. These sunken lanes are a common feature on the edge of the moor. Farmers would drive their cattle onto the moor for summer grazing and bring them down to lower levels in winter. Some still do.

Chagford was one of the four Stannary Towns of Dartmoor, where tin was brought to be assessed for quality, weighed and a tax paid on it. The last of the tin mines of the Chagford area, which closed in 1904, was at Great Weeke, towards the bottom of the lane, although there is not a lot to see now.

Once at Rushford Bridge the path is alongside a leat which goes to Rushford Mill. Rushford was mentioned in the Domesday Book and the old water-powered corn mill can still be seen alongside the stepping stones over the river. Chagford Bridge dates from about 1600 and crossing this leads to Factory Cross, so named because the large buildings here were once woollen mills.

The road back to the town, appropriately called Mill Street, is cut deeply into the rock and brings us to the square. A visit to the two hardware shops is a must. Owned by the same two families for several generations, you can buy just about anything there. Aladdin's caves, both of them.

THE BASICS

Distance: 3½ miles / 5.5km or 4½ miles / 7.25km

Gradient: One steep climb but otherwise not difficult

Severity: Moderate/Hard

Time: 2 hours or 2½ hours

Stiles: Three on the shorter walk, six on the longer walk

Map: OS Explorer OL28 (Dartmoor)

Path description: Footpaths, lanes and riverside paths. Possibly muddy in places.

Start point: Chagford town centre (GR SX 702874)

Parking: Pay and display car park in Chagford town centre (TQ13 8DP)

Dog friendly: Yes, but on leads if near animals on the moor or on public road

Public toilets: Chagford town centre

Nearest food: Several pubs and cafés in Chagford town centre

6 CHAGFORD WALK

THE ROUTE

1. Turn left out of the car park and then left again into New Street opposite the church (signed Postbridge). After passing a variety of old cottages there is a former pound for stray animals on the right. It has been made into a rest garden and there is an information board showing the panorama.

2. Shortly after the pound bear left up Nattadon Road. Just before the last houses at the top of the hill turn left up a rough and steep track signed Nattadon Common. Go through a gate and cross a small stream. Immediately go left up a steep path through the trees to reach an iron bench. (Do not follow the streamside path). The path is obvious as it climbs quite steeply to pass a second bench. The grassy path continues onwards and upwards with a stone wall on the left (possibly obscured by gorse and bracken in summer). Near the top, keep to the main grassy path veering slightly left to continue walking parallel to the wall. The views here are worth the effort. Chagford is now in the valley below and the massive bulk of Castle Drogo is visible across the Teign Gorge.

3. At a small car parking area turn right onto the lane. Ignore a lane on the right but turn left just before a sharp bend down a bridleway signed to Great Weeke. (Note: if you continue on the lane for another 150m you will come to Week Down Cross. This ancient cross probably marked the route of a medieval track across the moor from Chagford).

4. Follow the grassy path downhill with a stone wall on the left and enter an old drovers' lane down through the woods. Go through two gates and then a third at a path junction. This path may be muddy as it continues gently downhill towards Great Weeke.

5. At the bottom turn left on a tarmac lane. After 300m turn right by Westcott House signed Adley Lane.

6. Pass Adley House and just after a bungalow (Colene) turn left onto a footpath. The small footpath sign is on a wooden telegraph pole. Go over a stile and then cross the field diagonally right (do not go straight on alongside the hedge) towards a white house partially hidden behind some trees. Cross another stile by a gate and continue half right towards the same house and a third stile. The path goes

It is supposedly haunted by Lady Mary Howard, who allegedly murdered her four husbands and forever will have to ride out to Okehampton Park at midnight. Be warned! The ruins became popular with artists in the 19th century including J.M.W. Turner. It is in the care of English Heritage but closed in winter months. Back in Okehampton town centre the Museum of Dartmoor Life is also well worth a visit.

THE BASICS

Distance: 3 miles / 4.8km or 4 miles / 6.5km

Gradient: Fairly level

Severity: Easy

Time: 1½ or 2 hours

Stiles: None

Map: OS Explorer OL28 (Dartmoor)

Path description: Good surfaces, partly tarmac

Start point: White Hart Hotel, Fore Street, Okehampton (GR SX 587952)

Parking: Several pay and display car parks in Okehampton town centre. Some on-street parking (EX20 1JZ)

Dog friendly: Yes, but on leads where appropriate

Public toilets: Close to start and at Okehampton station (in season)

Nearest food: Several cafés and pubs in Okehampton. Café at Okehampton station on summer weekends

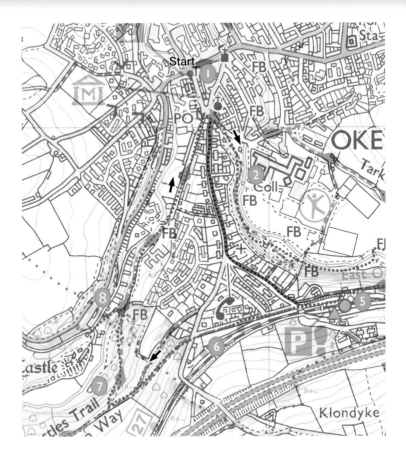

THE ROUTE

1. From the White Hart Hotel (a 17th-century coaching inn) go up George Street (Nat West Bank is on the corner). Pass Peel House (which was the old police station and has the toilets next door). Continue past Fairplace church on the left and ignore any turnings on the right. The road bends to the left and then 50m on the right is the entrance to Simmons Park.

2. Enter the park through the gates and follow the path alongside the East Okement River. Go past the lodge building, the Sidney Simmons memorial stone, the Swiss chalet and the small ornamental gardens. Cross the river on a bridge just before steps up to the station and with a children's play park on the left. Go immediately right to continue into Platt Meadow along the riverside path but now with the river on your right. The path goes around the Okehampton College sports grounds.

Ignore a bridge on the right and continue to a second bridge in the corner of the grounds. Cross the bridge and turn right.

3. At a path junction go through a gate and follow Ball Hill Footpath. At first this is alongside a meadow with a mill leat beside the path but soon it meets the river again.

4. Go through a gate onto a lane and turn right to pass under the stone railway viaduct. Cross the river on a timber bridge known as Charlotte's Bridge. (If

you wish, you can extend the walk by following the easy path upstream for half a mile or so before retracing your steps to this point). Otherwise, turn right here to go back under the viaduct and then through a gate. The path veers to the left and continues along the top of the meadow with the river below. Continue on this good track passing through two gates. Just after the second gate and opposite a stone house take some steps on your left up to Okehampton station.

5. After a look around this Southern Railway station with its small museum, continue out of the car park entrance to the road. Cross the road and go along the signed bridleway opposite. (If you wish, you can take the shorter option back to Okehampton town centre by turning right and following the road downhill). Otherwise, carry on and ignore side turnings to walk in front of a row of houses.

6. Cross another road at the end and take the footpath through a gate almost directly opposite. Go down through the woods, full of bluebells in spring. Ignore a side turning and carry on to meet another road.

7. Walk along this road for 100m and turn sharp right down the footpath signed for Okehampton Castle. (You will be able to see the ruins of the castle through the trees at this point.) Continue steadily down and ignore any side paths to reach a footbridge over the West Okement River. Cross the bridge, again signed Okehampton Castle, and immediately turn left. Shortly afterwards go right through a gate to a road. Go left up the road to the castle.

8. Retrace your steps and re-cross the timber bridge and now turn left to walk down the riverside path with the river on your left. Pass the old workhouse site (now sheltered accommodation). There is an interesting information board close to the exit onto Castle Road about the history of the buildings and the social conditions at the time it was established in 1836. Continue along Castle Road back to the town centre.

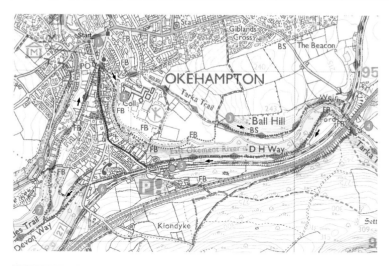

9 YES TOR & HIGH WILLHAYS

A MORE STRENUOUS WALK THAN OTHERS IN THE BOOK BECAUSE WE VISIT THE TWO HIGHEST TORS ON DARTMOOR, HIGH WILLHAYS AND YES TOR. THIS IS OPEN AND WILD DARTMOOR AND FROM THE SUMMIT WE CAN SEE DEEP INTO THE HEART OF THE MOOR.

Dartmoor has been used by the military for training purposes since Queen Victoria's time. Okehampton Camp, just below the parking area, is a military training facility managed by the Defence Training Estate, part of the MOD. In May it is the home of the annual Ten Tors challenge for teenagers.

The camp was built in the 1890s and many miles of tracks, known as military roads, were constructed for the movement of horse-drawn artillery. These roads remain and we will use one of them to get deep into the moor. At over 2000 ft (600m) this is the highest land in England south of the Peak District. Even then, Kinder Scout is only 48 ft (15m) higher.

Along the way we pass some disused rifle butts and the target railway that provided the moving targets. This was an unmanned railway. The engine was set in motion and pulled several trolleys, on which the targets were mounted, along the track, which had a loop at each end. Although this has not been used for many years the track and the engine house remain.

High Willhays and Yes Tor are effectively situated at either end of a short ridge between the East Okement and West Okement rivers. Yes Tor is the more impressive as tors go. Indeed, when you are there, it looks as if Yes Tor is the highest point and this was believed to be the case for many years before modern surveying techniques were available.

On Yes Tor you will see much of the high moor stretched before you with the communications mast on North Hessary Tor at Princetown providing a reference point. It can seem hard to believe at this remote and high place that it is only 25 miles (40km) to the sea at Plymouth to the south, Bude to the west or near Bideford to the north.

From Yes Tor we make our way down, carefully at first, to cross the Red-a-ven Brook to West Mill Tor some 78m (250 ft) below. Then it is an easy walk, although across open moor, to Rowtor (1535 ft or 468m) and back to the start.

NOTE: This walk is within the Okehampton Military Range Danger Area. You must check beforehand that no live firing is taking place. You can check online by putting 'Dartmoor Firing Programme' into your search engine or phoning 0800 458 4868. Red flags are flown from various points, including Yes Tor, if public access is not permitted.

PARKING: From Okehampton town centre follow signs to 'Camp'. After 1 mile pass the entrance to Okehampton training camp, go over a small bridge and up the hill for nearly a mile to the parking area at the top where the track forks.

THE BASICS

Distance: 5¼ miles / 8.5km

Gradient: No steep gradients but the first half is all uphill. One rather rough downhill section from Yes Tor

Severity: Hard. This walk is partly on open moorland, rough in places, and should not be attempted in poor visibility

Time: 3½ hours

Stiles: None

Map: OS Explorer OL28 (Dartmoor)

Path description: Stony military tracks and some open moorland. 4 streams to cross

Start point: Roadside parking area above Okehampton Camp (GR SX 596922)

Parking: See note above. (EX20 1QR)

Dog friendly: Yes, but on leads if near animals

Public toilets: None

Nearest food: Various options in Okehampton town centre

9 YES TOR & HIGH WILLHAYS WALK

THE ROUTE

1. Walk away from the parking area and take the right fork. There are views in every direction. The ridge of Belstone Tor is on the left and Rowtor on the right, behind which the flagpole on Yes Tor is visible.

    Note: If the flag is flying you should not be here!

2. After about 500m go right at a fork. After a further 650m pass old rifle butts on the left. Just after this carry straight on at a path crossing down to a ford.

3. However, if you look left at the path crossing you will see the embankment and engine house of the old target railway 200m away and easy to explore.

4. Turn left after the ford and continue onwards and upwards with West Mill Tor on the right. Bear right at the next fork and soon Yes Tor will appear ahead.

5. Cross another small stream and when you are almost at the summit bear left on a lesser track on a right-hand bend. (Yes Tor and its flagpole is on your immediate right here). Continue up the track towards the centre of three rock piles.

6. Pass these and two further outcrops become visible, one with a cairn on the top. This is High Willhays, the highest point on Dartmoor. The views are tremendous. Westwards is Great Links Tor with Bodmin Moor beyond. Ahead, in the distance, is Fur Tor (the most remote tor on the moor) whilst to the east is Steeperton Tor. The sea is visible on a good day and it is said that on occasions it is possible to see both the English Channel and the Bristol Channel from here.

7. Retrace your steps for 500m as far as the two outcrops that we passed earlier. Immediately before the rock pile bear left to see another paved track. Go right towards Yes Tor which, from this angle, appears to be higher than High Willhays.

8. Go left of the summit with the flagpole. The grey hut here seems rather out of place but is used by the military when firing takes place.

9. Leave Yes Tor with your back to the hut and with the flagpole on your right. Go carefully down the slope through the clitter (large blocks of granite), a bit of a scramble at first. Keep heading directly north-east towards West Mill Tor and a grassy path on the other side of the valley. Within five minutes or so a clear path will come into view below.

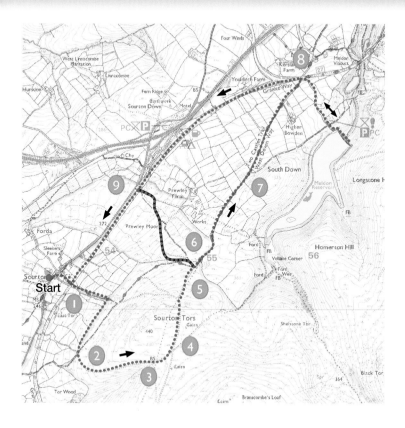

7. Go through the gate. (A shorter option to reach Meldon Reservoir dam is to bear right on the signed bridleway but it is rather rocky and can be muddy.) Go down the lane, at first stony and then tarmac, to a junction just before a railway bridge.

8. Turn right for the dam and walk along the lane for 600m. Go through the gate and pass a car park. Cross the dam to look down the steep-sided valley of the West Okement River towards the slender and graceful steel viaduct first opened in 1874. Retrace your steps back to the road junction and go straight across to join the former railway track. Turn left, noting the sculpture. There are several more on the way back.

9. Cross the road to the water treatment works by the cattle grid. It is just over 1 km (¾ mile) to Sourton church. At the church turn right just before the bridge and back to the car park.

11 GRIMSPOUND

THIS MOORLAND WALK IS STEEPED IN FIVE THOUSAND YEARS OF HISTORY. FROM THE WARREN HOUSE INN, THE HIGHEST PUB SOUTH OF THE PEAK DISTRICT, WE VISIT A BRONZE AGE SETTLEMENT, THE REMAINS OF A MEDIEVAL HAMLET AND REMNANTS OF 20TH-CENTURY TIN MINING.

The Warren House Inn stands at 434m (1425 ft) above sea level and there has been an inn here since at least 1755. There are several tales associated with this isolated place but it is claimed that the fire burning in the hearth has not been allowed to go out since 1845. There were three tin mine operations known as Birch Tor, Vitifer and Golden Dagger mines in the valley below until as late as 1930.

We start by walking towards Bennett's Cross where we will join the Two Moors Way. This ancient cross has the initials WB carved on it, indicating 'warren bounds', the boundary of Headland Warren, a commercial rabbit warren that was in existence until well into the 20th century.

After climbing gradually to the viewpoint of Hookney Tor with 360-degree views we will see Grimspound below. This is the best known of all the Bronze Age settlements on Dartmoor. The perimeter wall is over 500m (1650 ft) in circumference and inside are the remains of 24 huts and several animal pounds. It must have been a peaceful time as the site is sheltered and impossible to defend. It even has its own water supply with a stream running through.

We then pass the thatched farmhouse of Headland Warren and follow the stream, past ancient field systems on the hillside above, to the few remains of Challacombe medieval hamlet. Challacombe is mentioned in the Domesday Book and there were about seven houses and a mill here until about 1880 but only a few walls remain.

The path contours around Challacombe Down to the site of Golden Dagger mine which was the last working tin mine on Dartmoor. The story goes that it was named after a bronze dagger found nearby. Nature has reclaimed the site but the remains (some of which were still occupied in the 1940s) can still be seen.

Further up the valley we will see other ruins relating to Birch Tor mine. You can finish this walk with a visit to the Warren House Inn with plenty more tales of fact and fancy.

THE BASICS

Distance: 4 miles / 6.5km or 6 miles / 9.5km

Gradient: Fairly easy

Severity: Moderate

Time: 2 hours or 3 hours

Stiles: None

Map: OS Explorer OL28 (Dartmoor)

Path description: Moorland paths and tracks, some rocky and possibly wet in places

Start point: Kings Oven (GR SX 676811)

Parking: Small parking area just north of the Warren House Inn (2 miles north of Postbridge on B3212) (PL20 6TA)

Dog friendly: Yes, but on leads if near animals

Public toilets: None

Nearest food: Warren House Inn at start

11 GRIMSPOUND WALK

THE ROUTE

1. Walk along the roadside verge away from the Warren House Inn. This is a busy road but the verge is wide. After 600m there is another parking area. Cross this to go through a gap in the boundary towards an ancient cross. This is Bennett's Cross.

2. Bear right to pass the cross and bear left on to a sandy track, possibly muddy at times, up the hillside. Steadily climb, passing an old tinner's hut on the way. At the top there are splendid views towards Moretonhampstead and, slightly left, Castle Drogo standing proudly above the Teign Gorge. Cross a lane and continue on the bridleway through heather and whortleberries towards a stone wall.

3. Bear right to go through two gateposts and continue upwards away from the wall on a grassy path to reach Hookney Tor. Bear right to pass the first of the rock outcrops and then go left between the two main rock piles to descend on a path, rocky at first but then paved, to Grimspound. Across the valley you will be able to see the medieval strip fields on the hillside and old tinners' workings. Go into the Bronze Age settlement to explore the hut circles.

4. Leave Grimspound by the lower opening, the one you came in through, and down the grassy path, which soon becomes paved again. Cross a stream and continue towards the road. Turn left and after 250m turn sharp right down a tarmac track towards Headland Warren Farm to cross a cattle grid.

5. At this point the routes divide. To take the shorter route, continue along the drive. Shortly before the farmhouse you will see a sign diverting the bridleway behind the farm buildings. Go through the gate and follow the fence which passes the dog pound in which you can still see one of the kennels. At a footpath fingerpost carry straight on (signed Warren House Inn) with a stone wall on your left. Continue on this path which shortly brings you to the ruins of Birch Tor mine. Rejoin the instructions at waypoint 8.

    For the longer walk go left through the second of two metal gates, the one beside a ruined stone building. Pass some old corrugated iron buildings and continue on a grassy path alongside a barbed wire fence with old tin workings on the right. Continue along the valley to a gate by some large trees. Pass in front of the cottages and through a further gate leading onto a concrete track. The substantial ruins are all that is left of Challacombe medieval village.

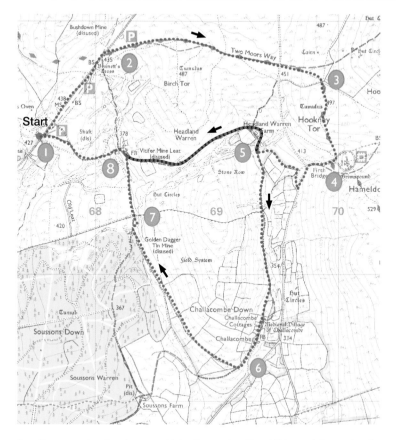

6. Pass a modern farmhouse and take the rough path uphill to reach two gates. Go through the right-hand gate signed as a footpath to Bennett's Cross. The grassy path shortly veers right up the valley with the Warren House Inn in the distance. Continue to a gate with a stile beside it and pass the remains of Golden Dagger mine. On the left you will see one of several buddles (for separating tin metal from the ore), then the site of an old generator house on the right, Dinah's house on the left and the waterwheel pits across the stream.

7. Go straight on at two path junctions and up a stony and often wet track.

8. At the remains of Birch Tor mine pass several ruins on the left and some enclosure walls on the right before turning left over a stream (do not go straight on at this point) and up the slope. Near the top, ignore a minor track on the left but bear left at the second fork to reach the car park.

12 POSTBRIDGE & BELLEVER

THE ANCIENT BRIDGE AT POSTBRIDGE IS ONE OF THE LARGEST OF DARTMOOR'S CLAPPER BRIDGES. FROM THE BRIDGE, THIS WALK TAKES US PAST BRONZE AGE BURIAL CHAMBERS AND OTHER PREHISTORIC REMAINS TO ONE OF THE FINEST VIEWPOINTS IN CENTRAL DARTMOOR.

The old clapper bridge over the East Dart River is believed to date from the 13th century and was on the medieval packhorse track from Chagford to Tavistock. Today's bridge beside it dates from the turnpike era and was built about 1790.

We take an easy forest track to the prehistoric settlement and ceremonial complex known by the delightful name of Kraps Ring. There is a walled enclosure and a dozen or so hut circles are still easily identifiable. There is also a stone row and a stone circle together with a splendid and unusual cist, or burial chamber, nearby.

We then follow a green track on the open moor to reach the summit of Bellever Tor, 443m (1453 ft) high. As it is one of the highest tors in the centre of the moor we get exceptional 360-degree views. On a clear day Sittaford Tor and Fernworthy Forest can be seen to the north, Haytor Rocks to the east, Holne Ridge to the south and Princetown with the communications mast on North Hessary Tor to the west.

After Bellever Tor we descend to the hamlet of Bellever. The track that we come down is on the route of the Lych Way, once known as the 'Corpse Way'. At one time parishioners in the area had, by law, to bury their dead at the parish church at Lydford, 12 miles away. The track across the moor still has numerous references to this with place names such as Coffin Wood and Corpse Lane.

There are two more bridges at Bellever. The substantial clapper bridge, although less complete than the one we saw at Postbridge, is still a fine old structure. It is thought that the gap in the middle never did have a granite top. Notches in the uprights suggest it may have had timber planks instead – they could be easily replaced after a flood.

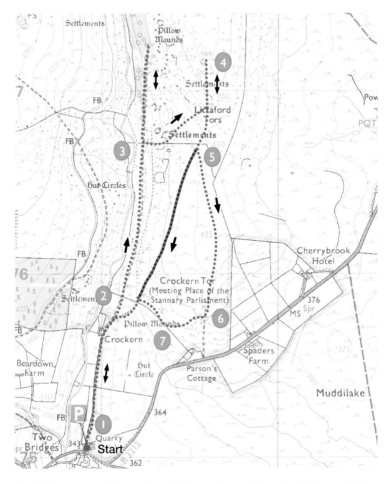

5. To visit Crockern Tor, bear left after the stile on a faint track, at first parallel to a stone wall and then veering away to the right. Soon you will see the insignificant outlying rocks of Crockern Tor with the main rocks on the slope beyond.

6. Go around the tor to the bottom right (southern) side where you will see the Parliament Rock where the Lord Warden of the Stannary Parliament is said to have taken his seat. Be careful, as it is rather rocky here. Now head down towards a boundary wall keeping the mast of North Hessary Tor straight ahead and the cottage on the left. At the wall, turn right. Ignore the first gateway opening and turn left through the second.

7. Bear right on an obvious path to meet the outward track and back to the car park.

14 PRINCETOWN

NO VISIT TO DARTMOOR WOULD BE COMPLETE WITHOUT A WALK FROM PRINCETOWN.

At times grey and forbidding, dominated by the prison and the communications mast on North Hessary Tor, it has a character of its own. At 435m (1430 ft) above sea level it is the highest village south of the Peak District.

Princetown was the brainchild of one man, Thomas Tyrwhitt. He was born in 1762 and had a privileged education. He became a secretary to the Prince of Wales (later to become George IV) who, as heir to the throne, was also Duke of Cornwall. To this day the Duchy of Cornwall own 27,300 hectares (67,500 acres) or nearly one third of the Dartmoor National Park.

Thomas Tyrwhitt had a vision of "improving" Dartmoor. He planned to tame the wilderness and exploit the natural resources of the moor. He wasn't a man to do things by halves and saw Dartmoor as a huge area of untapped wealth relatively close to the large naval port of Plymouth.

In 1785 he built a house for himself and named it Tor Royal. He then set about building walls to enclose moorland, constructing roads and quarrying stone. The village which appeared was named Princetown in honour of the Prince of Wales.

During the Napoleonic wars a large number of French prisoners were held in insanitary and overcrowded conditions in and around Plymouth and Thomas Tyrwhitt recommended that a war prison be built at Princetown. Work started in 1806 and quarries were opened for the vast quantities of granite needed.

The commercial value of granite was realised and a horse drawn tramway was constructed to transport the stone to Plymouth for shipment. The tramway reached Princetown in 1825 and in 1883 became a steam railway operated by the Great Western Railway.

There is hardly a more open or exposed village anywhere and it has been described as the "least suitable place that could ever have been chosen for a town". Eventually nature, with up to 80 inches of rain a year and sometimes more, together with the peaty and acid soil was the winner.

This walk takes us from the centre of the village along the route of the railway and to one of the larger quarries at Foggintor. From there we climb up to North Hessary Tor which is topped by a communications mast visible from many parts of Dartmoor and with 360° views.

THE BASICS

Distance: 4½ miles / 7km

Gradient: Fairly level but one undemanding climb to North Hessary Tor

Severity: Moderate

Time: 2¼ hours.

Stiles: None

Map: OS Explorer 28 Dartmoor

Path description: Old railway and tramways with an uneven climb on open moorland to North Hessary Tor. Should not be attempted in poor visibility

Start point: Princetown village centre. (GR SX 590735)

Parking: Pay and display car park in centre of Princetown. PL20 6QF

Dog friendly: Yes, but keep on leads when near animals

Public toilets: At start

Nearest food: Several pubs and cafés in Princetown

14 PRINCETOWN WALK

THE ROUTE

1. Turn left out of the car park entrance and just after the fire station bear left on a footpath signed as the Princetown Railway. The old brick and slate building, all that remains of Princetown station, was a stable for horses kept for local deliveries. The station itself was on the open area in front of the houses.

Beyond the conifer plantation views open up and it becomes obvious that the track is that of an old railway following the contours. On the left the sea can be seen at Plymouth Sound whilst on the right is the mast on North Hessary Tor which we visit later. Immediately ahead, the outlines of Leather Tor, Sharpitor and Leedon Tor are on the skyline.

As the track curves left it crosses a substantial bridge above an ancient tinners' workings and the head of the River Meavy. A little later, where the track changes direction towards the right, the hills of Bodmin Moor are visible on the horizon.

The track passes through a shallow cutting, where there are two granite posts inscribed PCWW 1917 which marked the limits of the catchment area of Burrator reservoir.

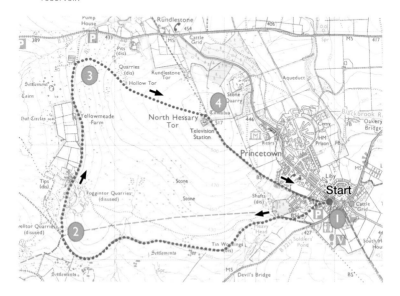

When a second bridge crosses another tinners' openwork, the estuary of the River Tamar is visible in the distance.

Continue for nearly half a mile and further sweeping right bend brings yet another panorama. Nearest is Swell Tor and its quarry, Ingra Tor in the middle distance and Great Staple Tor on the horizon.

2. Turn right at a path crossing onto a track towards Foggintor quarry. Pass granite waste tips and ignore the first opening into the quarry. Continue towards the ruins of several buildings including a row of cottages on what is known as Big Tip (for understandable reasons). Here you can go right to look into the quarry.

    Continue on the tramway path past more ruins, one of which was a chapel. Further on, there are walls enclosing fields and the granite setts on which the rails of the tramway were secured are obvious.

    Notice a granite post on the hillside which was a marker stone for an ancient track between Tavistock and Ashburton. There are others on the open moor nearby and, indeed, one is incorporated in the field wall.

3. Pass Yellowmeade Farm to reach a conifer tree on the site of what was once a row of cottages (and a track down to another small quarry). Turn right here up onto the open moor. Step across the leat, by a large boulder. Head across the open moor towards the communications mast on the skyline, but go slightly left initially to avoid some wet ground. The path is not clear at first but as Hollow Tor comes into view, it becomes clearer. Pass to the right of the tor and continue, uphill, towards the mast and the small rock outcrop which is North Hessary Tor. Go left of the mast to a gap in the fence in the corner by the wall. The trig point on the tor is at a height of 517 m (almost 1700 ft) above sea level. There are 365° views and it is worth pausing here.

4. Walk away from the tor following the stone wall on the left gently downhill towards Princetown. There are glimpses of the historic prison on the left and the tower of the parish church.

    At the bottom go through the gate onto a tarmac lane. Cross the entrance to Dartmoor Brewery and take the footpath to the right of a row of houses through trees.

    Turn left at the end and back to the cars.

15 MERRIVALE ANTIQUITIES

THIS EASY WALK EXPLORES THE PRINCIPAL FEATURES OF WHAT
HAS BECOME KNOWN AS THE MERRIVALE ANTIQUITIES. IT IS,
BEYOND DOUBT, THE FINEST PREHISTORIC SITE ON DARTMOOR,
CONVENIENTLY CLOSE TO A ROAD AND WITH SPLENDID VIEWS.

Much has been written about this magnificent Bronze Age ceremonial site. It has all the main elements you might hope to see with stone rows, a stone circle, standing stones, burial cairns and more than thirty hut circles. Near the start of the walk we will see the two parallel stone rows, an almost unique feature.

The area is surrounded by the remains of old industries and if you look around you will see evidence of granite quarrying to the left and right of the start point. It seems hard to imagine, but at its height in the mid-19th century, some 600 men were employed in Foggintor and Swell Tor quarries (looking towards the mast on the skyline). Merrivale (in the valley below) employed another 150 and there were 267 people living in the immediate area in 1861. There was quarrying here from 1820 to 1997 when the last Dartmoor granite quarry closed.

Granite for many well-known buildings came from this area, including Nelson's Column, the Houses of Parliament and, more locally, Dartmoor Prison. The stone for widening London Bridge, the one now in Arizona, came from the nearby Swell Tor Quarry.

The low walls by the parking area are all that remains of Foggintor school. It opened in 1915 with 55 pupils and closed as recently as 1936. Before demolition in the 1960s it became a private house, hence its name, 'Four Winds'.

As we head towards the Bronze Age remains you will see on your left King's Tor and the line of the old Plymouth to Princetown railway. In the distance we can see the Cornish skyline with Kit Hill and Bodmin Moor visible on a clear day.

On our way back we pass a large standing stone. Although it now appears to be in open moorland it is one of many erected in the 17th century to mark the route of a once busy packhorse track from Ashburton to Tavistock. You can still clearly see a letter 'T' incised on one side and an 'A' on the other. There is another such stone closer to Merrivale bridge and a further one on the slopes above Foggintor quarry in the distance.

THE BASICS

Distance: 2 miles / 3km

Gradient: Almost level

Severity: Easy terrain but on open moorland, should not be attempted in poor visibility

Time: 1 hour

Stiles: None

Map: OS Explorer OL28 (Dartmoor)

Path description: Grassy moorland tracks

Start point: Four Winds (GR SX 560749) on B3357 Tavistock to Princetown road just east of Merrivale

Parking: Free car park at start (PL20 6ST)

Dog friendly: Yes, but on leads where close to animals

Public toilets: None on walk but available in Princetown

Nearest food: Several cafés and pubs in Princetown, one mile away

15 MERRIVALE ANTIQUITIES WALK

THE ROUTE

1. With your back to the road go through the gap in the stone wall, past the prominent conifer and through another gap in the back wall. Turn right, do not cross the leat, but walk alongside on the grassy moorland.

2. Soon you will see the two stone rows ahead. Shortly before passing the large blocking stone at the end of each row, cross the leat on a tiny granite clapper bridge and walk alongside the left (longer) stone row. Stone rows are not uncommon on Dartmoor and we will see more on other walks in this book. To have two so close together is very rare indeed. The answer to the obvious question 'why?' will never be known for sure. After 75m you will see the large but broken capstone of a very good cist (burial chamber). A little further along the stone row is a ruined cairn.

3. Just beyond the end of the left stone row, turn right and go over a substantial bridge down a grassy path towards Great Mis Tor on the skyline ahead (and not towards the quarry to your left).

4. When you meet another broad grassy track coming up from the left, turn right up the slope. Here, mostly on the left but some on the right, are a large number of hut circles and larger pounds, in one of which you will find an abandoned apple crusher. Why this was left here and never finished is a mystery. After exploring the hut circles carry on up the grassy path bearing slightly to the right of the communications mast of North Hessary Tor. After 100m look out for the stone rows we followed earlier.

5. Cross the leat on the same clapper bridge as previously and turn right as far as the cist. Now bear left, again on a grassy path, towards the large standing stone and a small stone circle (although many of the stones are missing).

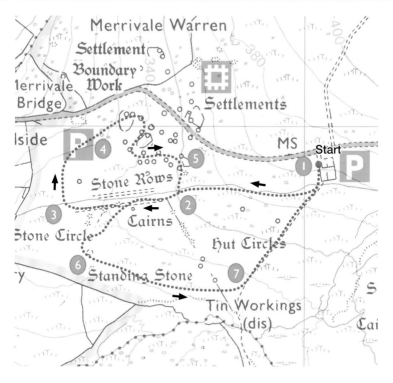

6. Turn left at the standing stone, again on a clear path towards the mast, and ignore any side turnings to the right. The line of the old railway is clear to see on our right. It was built by the Plymouth and Dartmoor Railway in 1823 and reached Princetown by 1825. Over a distance of 20 miles it climbed 1400 ft (425m)! Originally horse-drawn, the line was never profitable and was taken over by the GWR in 1883. It closed in 1956 but what a superb heritage railway it would make today.

7. At a grassy area where you can see a ford crossing the stream on your right, bear left up the slope towards another large standing stone and the trees of Four Winds beyond. This is the 'TA' stone mentioned earlier. Nearby you will be able to see unfinished dressed blocks of granite some of which clearly show the marks of the old way of splitting stone. Carry on towards the car park, crossing the leat on another small clapper bridge.

16 DOUBLE WATERS

THIS IS TRULY A WALK FOR ALL SEASONS ON THE WESTERN EDGE OF DARTMOOR. FROM THE LEVEL EXPANSE OF ROBOROUGH DOWN WE HAVE FAR-REACHING VIEWS BEFORE DROPPING INTO THE WOODED WALKHAM VALLEY.

This area is remarkably level. So much so, that at the southern end, just over a mile from the start point, there was a World War II airfield, known as RAF Harrowbeer, between the years 1941 and 1945.

At the start of the walk we have panoramic views towards Brent Tor, with its ancient church on the top, to the north. The church is dedicated to St Michael de Rupe, meaning St Michael of the Rock, and this is a common dedication for churches in high places. The legend has it that an early medieval merchant paid for it to be built after nearly being shipwrecked as this was the first land that he saw from his ship. Moving round we can see Cox Tor, Great Mis Tor, the communications mast on North Hessary Tor in the east and finally Sheep's Tor with Shell Top in the far distance to the south-east.

We use a well-surfaced track down to Double Waters where the rivers Walkham and Tavy meet. This was the location of the wonderfully named Virtuous Lady copper mine. Records of copper mining go back to 1558 and it was worked on and off until the 1870s. Part of the underground workings are under the river. The mine captain's house is still occupied today.

From there we follow the Walkham upstream and a more delightful riverside walk is hard to find. Passing reminders of former copper mining activity through oak woods we reach Grenofen Bridge, once the main route between the abbeys of Tavistock and Buckland. The shorter option returns up this ancient trackway but for a slightly longer walk we can carry on to meet the track bed of the former Tavistock to Plymouth railway. This passes over a splendid high level bridge above the river, known as Gem Bridge, named after another nearby mine, this time for tin. The bridge is now part of a long-distance cycle route, so beware of cyclists.

Gem Bridge was built in 2012 but the remains of the brick railway viaduct of 1910 (replacing an earlier Brunel viaduct) can still be seen. A short distance further on we cross another viaduct, known locally as Magpie Viaduct, built unusually of blue Staffordshire brick.

THE BASICS

Distance: 4½ miles / 7km or 6 miles / 9.5km

Gradient: Easy gradients but one steep ascent on the shorter option

Severity: Moderate

Time: 2 hours or 3 hours

Stiles: None

Map: OS Explorer OL28 (Dartmoor)

Path description: Mostly well-surfaced tracks, including a cycle path, and a riverside path. Parts of the riverside path may be muddy after rain.

Start point: Long Ash Garden Centre (signed from the A386 at Horrabridge) (GR SX 497694)

Parking: Parking area opposite the garden centre (PL20 7LL)

Dog friendly: Yes, but keep on leads when near animals

Public toilets: None

Nearest food: Moor T café at Long Ash Garden Centre

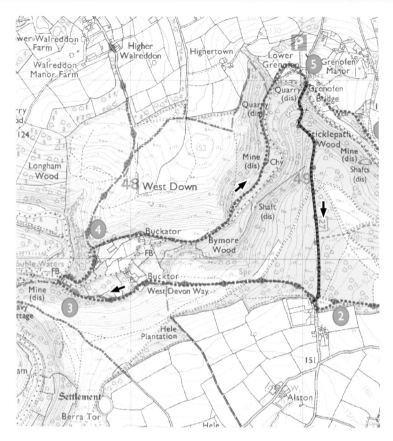

THE ROUTE

1. With the garden centre behind you, walk across the grassy moorland with a hedge on the left. After 100m cross a low bank and turn left, still with the field hedge on the left. Enjoy the splendid views across the moor. After about 200m turn left again onto a wide grassy track, again with a hedge on the left, to reach another parking area.

2. Go right on the track and then immediately bear left passing a 'Private Road' sign. This lane, with a wide grassy verge, drops steadily down with views across the wooded

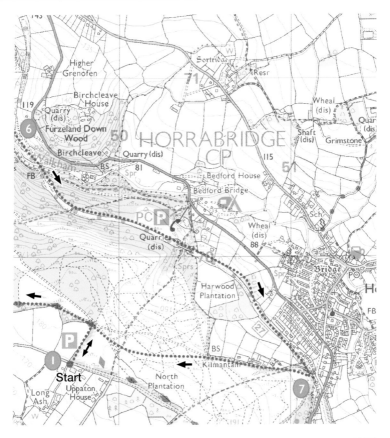

Walkham valley. The lane crosses a now dry leat which goes through a short tunnel under the lane. This leat was three miles long and supplied water to Lady Bertha and Virtuous Lady mines. As late as the 1950s it was also the water supply for the cottages at Double Waters. After passing the white gates to Bucktor the track becomes rather rough as it goes through woodland with the river soon visible on the right. At the bottom go down the slope to cross the footbridge over the River Walkham. The other river here is the Tavy. These are two of the fastest-flowing rivers in England.

3. After crossing the bridge go left of the large rock outcrop for just a few metres to find a gap on the right. Here it is a bit rocky and slippery for a very short distance but then take a clear track that leads away from the river and uphill to pass a cottage on the right. The path goes steeply left then right to meet another track.

4. Go right at the junction, signed as a public bridleway. This goes downhill to pass behind a second cottage before dropping down to the riverside again. Continue along the path with the river on the right and after a while pass a mine chimney and other remains of West Down copper mine. Although the rock in the valley is a hard greenish grey slate, granite is not far below the surface and this is where the copper, tin and other minerals are found. Go through a gate, passing behind Lower Grenofen to reach a lane.

5. For the shorter walk, go right over the ancient bridge and zigzag up a fairly steep and rather rocky path. As it levels out it becomes grassy and after about 500m reaches the parking area we passed earlier at waypoint 2 above. Turn left and return to the car park, keeping the hedge boundary on the right.

   Otherwise cross the lane and go through a wooden gate signed Drakes Trail. The path goes through a meadow before reaching another gate, then winds up between trees to reach the old Plymouth to Tavistock railway.

6. Turn right on the cycle track. For the next 1½ miles (2.5km) this is a shared track with cyclists. Go over Gem Bridge which is 24m (79 ft) above the River Walkham. Soon Magpie Viaduct is reached. At one time the Magpie Inn stood on the road below, hence the name. The track enters a development of modern houses on the site of Horrabridge station (note the house names!) to reach a cattle grid.

7. Immediately go very sharp right, almost doubling back, up a good track passing several houses on the right. After the last one (Kilmantain), the track becomes grassy. Bear left uphill and go slightly right at the top. Look for two benches on the left with a low grassy bank behind them. Turn left over the bank to the car park.

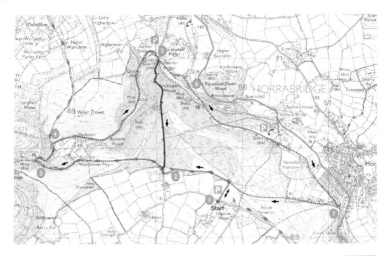

17 BURRATOR RESERVOIR

BURRATOR IS SURELY ONE OF THE MOST BEAUTIFUL RESERVOIRS IN ENGLAND. FROM THE END OF THE RESERVOIR WE CLIMB TO THE LEGENDARY CRAZYWELL POOL, THEN WALK HIGH ABOVE THE LAKE BEFORE RETURNING ALONGSIDE THE WOODED WATER'S EDGE.

Burrator is Plymouth's main water supply. As early as the late 16th century, Sir Francis Drake, hero of the Spanish Armada, is credited with bringing a water supply from the River Meavy along a channel, known as the Plymouth Leat. This leat, sometimes called Drake's Leat, started at what is now the head of the reservoir and was a little over 17 miles long. The reservoir itself was completed in 1898 and expanded by raising the height of the dam in 1928.

We then visit Crazywell Pool on the longer walk. This is a mysterious place and it is probably a remnant of tinners' diggings from Tudor times. There are several legends associated with it, and one says that it is bottomless!

Nearby is Crazywell Cross. This is one of a series of crosses that are on the line of an ancient trackway across the moor. This path is often called the Abbots Way as it linked the monastic centres of Buckfast in the east and Buckland and Tavistock abbeys in the west. Like a lot of other things on Dartmoor there is no certainty that this is the route taken by the monks but there is no doubt that such a path did exist.

The east–west crossing of the moor was also important for other reasons. Ashburton, less than two miles from Buckfast Abbey, and Tavistock were both Stannary towns, i.e. centres for the ancient tin industry. Both these towns were also important for the wool trade. There is another cross just visible 500m away to the east and we will pass a third at Cross Gate later on the walk.

Soon we walk beside the Devonport Leat. We meet this water channel on other walks. It was constructed in the 1790s to supply the naval town of Devonport because its neighbour, Plymouth, would not agree to share their water supply. Today the Devonport Leat is a major part of Plymouth's water supply and there is an impressive waterfall near the dam where water from the leat tumbles into Burrator Reservoir. We finish this walk by following a path through the trees and along the edge of the lake.

THE BASICS

Distance: 4 miles / 6.5km or 5 miles / 8km

Gradient: Easy gradients

Severity: Moderate

Time: 1¾ hours or 2½ hours

Stiles: One (but can be avoided)

Map: OS Explorer OL28 (Dartmoor)

Path description: Moorland tracks, stony in places, a quiet lane and woodland paths

Start point: Norsworthy Bridge (GR SX 568693) From Burrator reservoir dam follow signs to Arboretum car park and then take right fork signed Norsworthy Bridge

Parking: Free parking area close to bridge (PL20 6PE)

Dog friendly: Yes, but on leads if near animals on the moor or on public road

Public toilets: Close to reservoir dam

Nearest food: Burrator Inn at Dousland or Royal Oak at Meavy, both 1 mile from the start

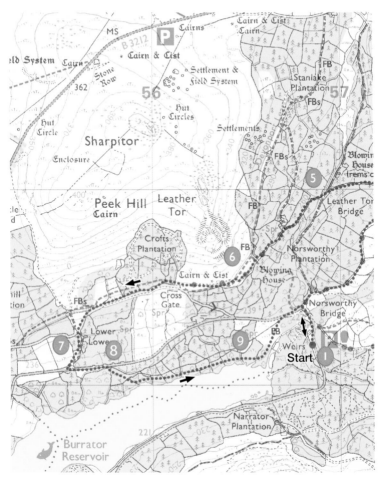

THE ROUTE

1. From the parking area go back to Norsworthy Bridge. Turn immediately right up the stony track.

At a path junction bear right and after just a short distance you will see a solitary large boulder beside the track. An attempt to split this has failed but the old way of feather and tare is clear to see. A row of holes has been drilled and the iron feather and tare, a form of wedge which was hammered to split the rock, is stuck in one of the holes. Perhaps this is why it was abandoned.

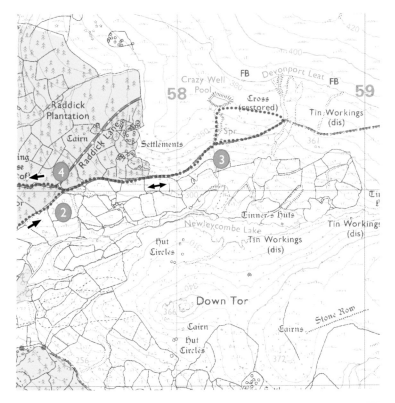

2. At a second junction continue uphill on the wide track to visit Crazywell Pool. Otherwise turn left here and follow the route from waypoint 5.

On the right are the old field boundaries of Kingsett Farm which was abandoned along with several others when Burrator reservoir was built. Some ruined farm buildings can be seen as well as the field walls. Once on the open moor the track climbs gradually and Crazywell Cross can be seen silhouetted on the skyline.

3. At a bend in the track, cross a small stream from a tinner's gulley and go immediately left up a rough pathway. This quickly becomes a grassy track following the gully. At the top is Crazywell Pool, hidden until almost the last moment.

From the pool go right towards the cross and continue past it to meet the main track again.

Turn right to go back down, retracing your steps, with views of Down Tor and Sheep's Tor on the left and the reservoir beyond.

4. Turn right at the first junction and go down to Leather Tor bridge. You can see that this was originally an old clapper bridge and that the parapets were added later.

5. Turn right here to cross over the bridge and shortly afterwards on the right is a potato cave with the ruins of Leather Tor Farm behind. The cave would have been used for storing potatoes and other root crops.

6. Continue uphill, (ignoring side turnings) and cross the Devonport Leat at the top. Turn left and after 50m look out for a very good example of a cist or burial chamber on the right (surrounded by a wooden fence).

Walk alongside the leat to meet a lane and another old cross by the junction (known as Cross Gate). There are views across Burrator reservoir towards the dam.

Follow the lane alongside the leat for about 600m. Shortly after the point where the leat crosses under the road again you will see a ruined building of Lower Lowery Farm .

7. Turn left down a broad track to pass the building and continue down to meet the reservoir perimeter road.

8. Turn left again and after about 200m go right over a stile beside a gate into the woodland. (Continue along the road to avoid the stile if you prefer, but beware of traffic).

Go immediately left and walk alongside a high deer fence on the left to reach a path junction by a grassy area beside the lake. Go left through a gate and continue on a woodland path with the fence now on the right.

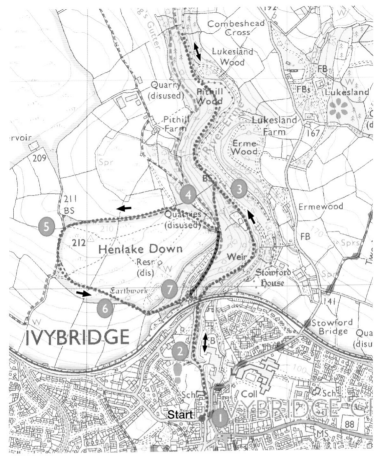

5. Just before the field boundary with a metal gate ahead turn left (but stop to see the views across the fields towards the sea and Plymouth Sound). Where the path divides, bear left to walk along a fairly level path with Ivybridge visible below on the right.

6. The path descends to a gate in the corner. Go through the gate and down through some mixed woodland. You reach the lane again just after a short tunnel.

7. Turn right and walk down the hill and under the viaduct. Continue on the lane (past Victoria Park on the right with its children's playground) and back to Station Road and the start point.

19 VENFORD RESERVOIR

VENFORD IS ONE OF THE SMALLER RESERVOIRS OF DARTMOOR. IT IS SET IN AN AREA OF THE MOOR SURROUNDED BY HUT CIRCLES, CAIRNS, STONE ROWS, SEVERAL ANCIENT WATER CHANNELS AND EVIDENCE OF MINING ACTIVITIES.

We start this walk with a level path around the reservoir itself which will only take 45 minutes. In spring there are bluebells close to the water's edge followed later by non-native rhododendrons which make a colourful display reflected in the water.

The reservoir was constructed to supply water to the growing seaside resort of Paignton and was completed in 1907. Several granite posts with the initials PUDC (Paignton Urban District Council) will be seen along the route. Other posts with the initials RDH denote the boundary of the original owner of the land, Richard Dawson of Holne.

After passing the modern water treatment works we follow an easy track beside the Venford Brook as it leaves the reservoir to join the River Dart. Water for domestic use is piped to Paignton under this track and remnants of pipes can be seen.

We enter an ancient moss-covered oak wood before climbing, fairly steeply near the top, to Bench Tor, 323m (or just over 1000 ft) above sea level. The climb is worth the effort as the reward is a 360-degree panorama over the Dart Gorge 500 ft (150m) below. On a clear day the views extend deep into the moor whilst in the opposite direction the sea can be seen beyond the South Devon countryside.

There is evidence of human activity over thousands of years. Just below Bench Tor are the remains of an ancient homestead whilst soon we cross the Holne Moor Leat, sometimes known as Hamlyn's Leat. This leat is 4½ miles long and was built by the Hamlyn family at the very beginning of the 19th century to provide a reliable source of water to their woollen mills at Buckfastleigh. Higher Buckfast Mill is no longer working but both it and the leat, still carrying water, can be seen in the grounds of Buckfast Abbey.

Another leat, even longer at over 9 miles, is almost parallel to the Holne Moor Leat and was for the Wheal Emma copper mine near Buckfastleigh. Although now dry, its route can still be followed on the moor.

THE BASICS

Distance: 1 mile / 1.5km or 3 miles / 4.5km

Gradient: The short walk is level. The longer walk has one short steep climb

Severity: Short walk: Easy. Longer walk: Moderate with one short steep climb

Time: 45 minutes or 1¾ hours

Stiles: None

Map: OS Explorer OL28 (Dartmoor)

Path description: Moorland paths and tracks. Partly on open moorland and should not be attempted in poor visibility

Start point: Venford Reservoir (GR SX 685713)

Parking: Car park on northern side of reservoir dam (TQ13 9UG)

Dog friendly: Yes, but on leads if near animals on the moor

Public toilets: At start

Nearest food: Cafés at Dartmeet and Holne, each about 2 miles distant. Pub at Holne

19 VENFORD RESERVOIR WALK

THE ROUTE

1. Leave the car park at the lower end, closest to the dam, and cross the road where you will see the first of the RDH stones. Follow the railings on the left for 50m and then go through a metal gate into the woodland. Notice the mortar stone on the left just inside the gate, a reminder that tin was a major industry in the area until as recently as the 19th century. Follow the easy level path through the mixed woodland along the edge of the reservoir lake. Several streams empty into the lake at the top end. Cross over a wooden bridge and go left. The path can be a little muddy at this point but will soon improve as we walk back towards the dam.

2. Follow the path through the trees but beware of the tree roots which can be a hazard. Ignore the gate by the steps but look for another gate in the railings on the right about 25m before the end of the stone parapet of the dam. Go left on the road noticing one of the PUDC boundary markers opposite. Cross the dam to complete the shorter walk.

3. For the longer walk do not cross the dam but pass the entrance to Venford Water Treatment Works and walk on the moorland with the railings on the left. At the corner of the railings, where there is another PUDC marker stone, go left down the slope, keeping the railings on the left. At the bottom turn right onto a good track with the Venford Brook on the left. This stone-edged pathway is the pipe track and as it descends gently Sharp Tor will soon appear on the horizon ahead.

4. After a while the track contours around the hill into an oak wood and passes a fenced area on the left. Where it starts to bend quite sharply to the right look out for two prominent large granite slabs on the right. At this point turn right up a minor track through the ancient woodland with moss-covered trees and boulders. Be careful as there is no sign and if the main track has straightened out you have gone too far. As the path emerges from the woodland onto the open moor it steepens as it climbs to reach Bench Tor.

5. There are fantastic views over the Dart Gorge. On a clear day the sea near Torbay can be seen ahead whilst behind is Princetown and the communications mast on North Hessary Tor. A good place to rest and enjoy the Dartmoor scenery. Return to the top of the path that you came up. With the rocks of Bench Tor on the left go past two hawthorn trees over the grassy moor heading slightly left of the

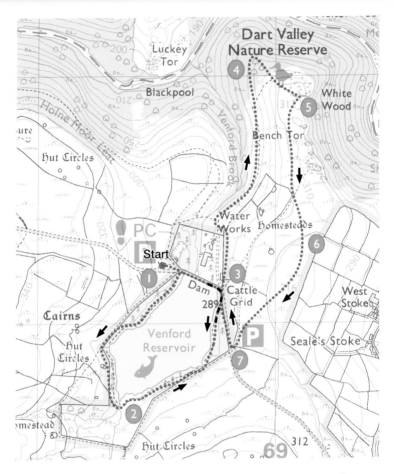

reservoir ahead. At first the path is not obvious but as it descends past a few more scattered hawthorn trees and rocky outcrops on the left it becomes clearer. The path bends to the left and climbs slightly towards a telephone pole on the skyline shortly before reaching a stone field wall.

6. Go half right by the pole over the Holne Moor Leat and then right on a sandy track which soon becomes grassy. The path divides after a few metres. Take the right fork bearing away from the wall and towards the conifers surrounding Venford Reservoir.

7. Cross the leat again and follow the wide grassy path to reach a parking area. Turn right to follow a path along the verge beside the road to the dam. Cross the dam and back to the car park.

20 NEW BRIDGE

NEW BRIDGE WAS NEW IN THE EARLY 15TH CENTURY AND
IS ONE OF THE LOWEST CROSSING POINTS OF THE RIVER
DART BEFORE IT LEAVES DARTMOOR. WE START THE WALK IN
UNUSUAL FASHION BY GOING THROUGH ONE OF THE THREE
GRANITE ARCHES.

It is a popular spot with walkers and canoeists or those who just want a relaxing afternoon.
It is possible to walk both upstream and downstream of the bridge almost alongside the
river and this in itself makes for a relaxing stroll. The beginning of this walk is upstream
across an area known as Deeper Marsh although it is not at all marshy.

Deeper Marsh is one of the few areas on Dartmoor where the Brimstone butterflies
thrive. Although bright yellow, the underside of their folded wings provides such excellent
camouflage that they become invisible when at rest.

The whole area was once part of the Manor of Spitchwick. The best remembered owner
was a certain Dr Blackall who lived at Spitchwick in the late 19th century. He was a
prominent doctor in Exeter and obviously a man of some substance. He had the drive built
so that he could enjoy the views over the Dart Gorge from the comfort of his own carriage.

To this day the track is shown on
maps as Dr Blackall's Drive. It is 1½
miles (2.5 km) from the top near Bel
Tor to the bottom where it meets the
Ashburton to Princetown road.

Our walk follows the riverside to the
gatehouses at the end of the drive
to Spitchwick Manor (still owned by
descendants of Dr Blackall). We then
climb up through woodland to Leigh
Tor, one of the lesser-known Dartmoor
tors but impressive nevertheless.

Crossing the road we are now almost at the end of Dr Blackall's Drive and if you want to
extend this for views over the wooded gorge you can follow the track as it twists and turns
above the river valley. Although too far for a 'walk for all ages' from New Bridge there is a
car park at the top of the hill at Bel Tor Corner.

So instead we drop down below the drive, passing a quarry from which the stone for the track may have come. After following a path on the moorland we descend through heather and bracken to join a good track through a nature reserve and back to the river again at New Bridge.

THE BASICS

Distance: 3 miles / 4.8km

Gradient: Level to start, followed by a fairly steep uphill and an easier descent

Severity: Easy at first, then Moderate but with a steep uphill section

Time: 1¾ hours

Stiles: None

Map: OS Explorer OL28 (Dartmoor)

Path description: Grassy moorland paths with some bracken in summer, otherwise paths and good tracks

Start point: New Bridge (GR SX 711709)

Parking: Car park at start. Honesty box and suggested donation of £1 (TQ13 7NX)

Dog friendly: Yes, but on leads if near animals on the moor

Public toilets: At start

Nearest food: Tavistock Inn at Poundsgate. Cafés, shops and pubs in Ashburton

1. Walk out of the car park past the honesty box and across the lane signed to Hannaford. Bear left on the footpath signed as the Two Moors Way to Deeper Marsh, which goes down several steps and then under the arch of New Bridge. The Two Moors Way is a long-distance path that crosses Devon from north to south across Exmoor and Dartmoor and is 103 miles long. After the bridge walk along the riverside path, fenced on the left. Cross a small stream and go right up a slope beside a wire fence. The path climbs above the river and then bears right dropping fairly steeply back down again towards an open grassy   area, a favourite picnic spot. This is Deeper Marsh, which is not marshy at all, but nice easy turf beside the River Dart. It is along here where you may be lucky to spot the Brimstone butterflies in spring and summer. The males are bright yellow although females are a paler colour altogether. Follow the river around to the left and cross a slight depression, which sometimes fills with water. A short detour on the path to the left here will bring you to the rather overgrown remains of an Iron Age pound. This was probably to protect livestock from predators. Otherwise, continue with the river on your right.

2. When the river swings sharply right the footpath meets a minor lane. Turn right, still walking beside the river.

3. Just before the two gatehouses turn sharp left by several big boulders. There is no footpath sign here although it is still on the route of the Two Moors Way. The gatehouses are at the bottom of the drive which leads up to Spitchwick Manor, once the home of Dr Blackall. The footpath climbs gently at first alongside a stone wall and fence. The gradient increases as the path veers to the left onward and upward, through bracken in summer months, to reach Leigh Tor. This is a good point to catch your breath and to see the views behind of Top Tor and Pil Tor in the general direction of Widecombe. Slightly to the left of them is the tower of Leusdon church, where Dr Blackall is buried.

4. The path climbs a little more to reach the main Ashburton to Princetown road. Cross this carefully and bear right on a grassy track to meet a tarmac lane. Behind is now the distinctive conical summit of Buckland Beacon where the Ten Commandments can be found carved on two huge granite slabs. But that is another story!

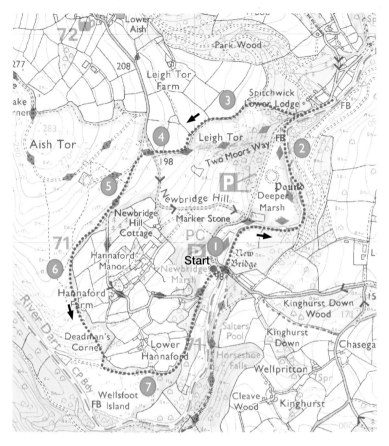

5. Turn left down the lane with views ahead over the Dart Valley and Holne Moor beyond. On a left-hand bend beside a stone wall continue straight on along a grassy track. Follow this track with a stone wall and a fence on the left and open moorland on the right.

6. Ignore two side paths but fork left at the corner. Keep close to the stone wall and fence on the left to drop steadily downhill. It is a bit stony for a while as it drops more steeply towards the bottom.

7. Turn left at the flat area and follow the easy and level woodland track through a nature reserve to meet a minor lane. The old field walls on the left are completely covered in moss. Turn right onto the lane to get back to the car park but before you do, have a look over the iron railings on the left at the magnificent lily pond.

ABOUT THE AUTHOR

John Noblet spent much of his childhood in the shadow of Dartmoor. From an early age his parents encouraged him to go walking and to take an interest in the countryside around their home. It is, therefore, entirely appropriate that John was approached to compile this book of walks for all ages.

His working life has taken him around the country and at one time or another he has lived near or walked in almost every English and Welsh National Park. He now lives again on the edge of Dartmoor and is active with several walking and local interest groups.